Mighty Mike
Bounces Back

For my family: whose love, encouragement,
and support help me pursue my dreams.

And to Mighty Mike Simmel: You asked me to write
your story and I learned good deeds do bounce back.
Keep inspiring and dribbling!

—RS

◦ ◦ ◦

For my parents, Bill and Joanne,
whose love and encouragement were always there
to pick me up when I fell down.

—MS

Mighty Mike Bounces Back

A Boy's Life With Epilepsy

by Robert Skead
and Mike Simmel

Magination Press ◉ Washington, DC
American Psychological Association

jj
skead
PRS

Published by
Magination Press
An Educational Publishing Foundation Book
American Psychological Association
750 First Street, NE
Washington, DC 20002

For more information about our books, including a complete catalog, please write to us, call 1-800-374-2721, or visit our website at www.magination-press.com.

Cover and book design by Kathy Keler
Cover photograph by PM Images/Getty Images

Printed by Worzalla, Stevens Point, WI
Library of Congress Cataloging-in-Publication Data
Skead, Robert.
  Mighty Mike bounces back : a boy's life with epilepsy / by Robert Skead & Mike Simmel.
    p. cm.
  Summary: Mike, who has had epilepsy since the age of two, copes with the challenges posed by his condition with the help of his understanding parents, caring doctors, and his love of basketball. Includes author's notes.
  ISBN-13: 978-1-4338-1043-5 (hardcover)
  ISBN-10: 1-4338-1043-3 (hardcover)
  ISBN-13: 978-1-4338-1042-8 (pbk.)
  ISBN-10: 1-4338-1042-5 (pbk.)
  [1. Epilepsy--Fiction. 2. Basketball--Fiction. 3. Schools--Fiction.] I. Simmel, Mike. II. Title.
PZ7.S62582Mi 2012
[Fic]--dc22
                            2011011081

Nov. 2011

Manufactured in the United States of America

10 9 8 7 6 5 4 3 2

Contents

Prologue

Mighty Mike took the pass from his teammate and raced the ball to the hoop. Within seconds his defender guarded him tightly. Mike faked right, spun as he dribbled between his legs, and left his defender in his wake. Suddenly, another guard covered him like a glove.

Mike had always dreamed about a moment like this. He glanced up at the scoreboard. It was the fourth quarter of the game. His team was down by one point.

The clock counted down...10, 9, 8...

Mike froze for a moment. He knew his parents were watching him from the stands. And at that moment, Mike felt as if he and his parents shared one mind. They all knew that it had been a long and hard journey for Mike to get to where he was right now—a star on his town's travel basketball team. Along the way, the pint-sized sharpshooter had earned a new nickname—Mighty Mike—a name that reflected his courage and determination more than his physical strength.

Mike also knew that his doctor was in the stands watching. Mike's journey had gifted him with so many people who cared for and helped him. But best of all was the fact that he knew his parents, teammates, coach, counselor, and doctor were all thinking the same thing. *You've come a long way, dude,* he thought to himself.

Mike waited as his teammate picked his defender. He dribbled by him and dished the ball to another teammate who cut to the hoop. Seconds later, the ball was flicked back into Mike's hands. He stopped and froze.

"Three! Two!" The crowd shouted...

Can't Hop

Mike watched his friends as they rode their bikes up and down the block. The scrawny boy with short pants brushed the hair out of his face. Each time the boys drove by, tears welled up in his dark brown eyes. Soon the boys had jumped off their bikes and started a game of tag. They ran like crazed monkeys away from Vinnie, another six-year-old boy with a nest full of unkempt red hair. Vinnie wore jeans with a hole in the knee and a New York Yankees t-shirt. Mike studied one of the boys, who was hopping backwards trying to keep Vinnie from tagging him. From where he stood across the street, Mike tried to copy the hop, but he fell to the ground.

"I *can't* do anything," called Mike to his mom. He picked himself up, bent his knees, and launched himself forward this time. Again, he tumbled hard to the ground. "See. I can't do it."

Across the street, Vinnie saw Mike fall on the grass and laughed. His laughter rippled through the air and went straight to Mike's heart. Vinnie had been one of Mike's friends, but he never seemed to ask to play with Mike anymore.

"Mike can't ride a bike," said Vinnie to one of the other boys, just loudly enough that Mike could hear him.

Mike peered across the street and saw the boys staring at him. He turned his head quickly so they couldn't see a tear run down his cheek. He jogged inside.

Mike's mom sighed. She had a thin nose and short black hair with blonde highlights. She threw a look to the boys across the street, letting them know she wasn't happy, and then followed Mike into their grey-paneled house. She found Mike on the living room couch with his head stuck under a pillow. He looked like a short ostrich with his head in the ground and his hiney in the air. She sat down beside him. "I know you're frustrated," she said. "But you're developing at a different pace because of your epilepsy. You'll be able to ride a bike and do lots of other things someday."

Mike hated that word: epilepsy.

Epilepsy is a physical disability and the result of a **seizure disorder.** A **seizure** is when someone's brain starts doing abnormal things that, among other things, can cause the person to lose consciousness. Some people with epilepsy will stare into space, some fall to the ground like rag dolls, and some can even fall down and shake. When he was young, Mike often had the kind of seizure that made him fall to the ground—and he couldn't control it. Seizures can happen any time, and in most cases, without warning. Seizures and epilepsy aren't contagious like a cold or flu. For people who have epilepsy, seizures are a part of life.

Mike had his first seizure at age two. It happened while he was eating an English muffin in the kitchen. His body went limp like cooked spaghetti, he fell off a stool, and he hit the floor hard. Because nothing like this had ever happened to Mike before, his mom did the right thing and called 911 immediately. When the emergency medical technicians arrived at his house and looked in his eyes, they knew Mike had experienced a seizure.

The next day, Mike's parents took him to the doctor, where they all learned about epilepsy. That same day, Mike had more seizures. They happened every day. The seizures scared Mike. They would come at any time, whether he was at home or in a public place, like a store. And he experienced them several times a day. Each time, the seizure would cause him to suddenly black out and drop to the ground.

Mike's mom gently moved the pillow that Mike was hiding under and stroked his black hair. "It's all right, honey." Mike enjoyed his mom's gentle caress. He remembered how the doctor told them that seizures are like lightning bolts going off in his brain. He was tired of feeling afraid of when the next one might happen. *Why'd this have to happen to me?* he thought.

Chapter 2

Helmet Head and Picnic Dinners

Mike's mom and dad did everything they could to protect him when seizures happened. One day, Mike fell so hard on the ground during a seizure that he cut his head. To help make sure that wouldn't happen again, his mom and dad bought a bicycle helmet for Mike's head. He wore the helmet almost all the time.

"I hate this helmet! It feels weird!" Mike complained. "People stare at me," he said, as his mom strapped it on.

"They stare at you because you're so handsome," answered his mother.

"They stare at me because I have a stupid helmet on," replied Mike.

"Ha," chuckled his mom. "I think it's because you're so cute." She gave him a smile. "Go outside and play."

Mike walked outside to his driveway. He noticed Vinnie shooting baskets on a mini-basketball hoop at his house across the street. "Hey! Did you get a bike?" shouted Vinnie, noticing Mike's helmet.

"No," answered Mike.

"Why're you wearing that helmet then?" asked Vinnie.

Mike wished he could erase epilepsy from his life. He thought about explaining the helmet to Vinnie, but he knew his parents had already talked to everyone in the neighborhood about it. Mike ignored the question. He took out his colored chalk, sat down on the driveway, and started drawing.

I hate this helmet, thought Mike. He unsnapped the clasp, took the helmet off his head, and threw it onto the grass. Feeling lighter, he turned his attention back to drawing.

"Mike! Put that helmet back on!" It was his mother. She walked toward him anxiously.

"No." Mike didn't even look up at her.

Mike's mom picked up the helmet and brought it to him. "You're on a cement driveway. What if you have a seizure?" she asked.

"Don't care." Mike still didn't look up at her.

"Michael, you know that if something bad were to happen right now you could cut your head again. We need to be safe. Put the helmet on." Mike's mom sounded like she meant business.

Mike pressed the chalk into the driveway harder. "Don't want to. I hate it."

"You will put on that helmet, and do you know why you're gonna do it?" said his mom.

"Because you'll give me a time out if I don't?" whispered Mike, finally looking up.

"No—because we'll have ice cream for dessert if you do," she replied.

A half smile appeared on Mike's face. He looked up at her. At first his eyes asked, "Do you mean it?" He could tell from the look on her face that she wasn't joking. "Two scoops?"

"All right. Two scoops," she agreed. She bent down, placed the helmet on his head, and secured the clasp faster than Mike could make a face about it.

As Mike's parents and his older brother Joe learned to live with epilepsy, they found many ways to protect him. They even ate breakfast, lunch, and dinner on the floor, picnic-style, away from the hard-edged table. And they used plastic utensils.

Mike enjoyed eating on the floor—it was fun! His mom served his favorite foods. And there was always that extra scoop of chocolate ice cream for dessert, which was great!

Mike's epilepsy also meant that he had to be in special gym classes in school. But for Mike, the hardest part about having epilepsy was that he was always a little different from everyone else.

Chapter 3

Taking Chances

"We don't want him to play with us," said Tommy to Mike's big brother Joe. Tommy wore blue jeans and a white t-shirt. His dark tan made his white-blond hair seem even whiter.

"Yeah, why does he always have to tag along? I don't want to catch eflipipsy, or whatever it's called," exclaimed Johnny, a 10-year-old boy with brown hair.

Joe glanced over at Mike, who stared at the ground. "It's epilepsy, Johnny, and I've told you already: You can't catch it, so quit asking. He's coming along because he's my brother, that's why. He's ok, guys. Forget he's eight. Come on Mike. You can be on my team." The smile jumped from Joe's face to Mike's as his big brother showed him how to hold the Wiffle ball bat correctly.

"You don't need a helmet to play Wiffle ball," sneered Vinnie.

"Mike does," chimed Kristin, Mike's next-door neighbor. Kristin was the girl in the neighborhood all the boys liked being friends with. Her hair was the exact color of a brown crayon. "I think he looks great in it too."

Kristin's words caused Mike to turn red.

"Go play outfield, Vinnie," said Joe, grasping the Wiffle ball in his hand and finding the right grip so the ball wouldn't curve. "I'm pitching to my brother."

Vinnie huffed and placed himself strategically only ten feet behind Joe. Mike knew that meant Vinnie didn't think he'd hit the ball very far, if he even hit it at all.

Joe winked at his brother and tossed the ball underhand. Mike swung hard and missed the pitch by a country mile. Joe pitched the ball again, only this time he tried to hit the bat with the ball so Mike could get a hit. But Mike missed the next eight pitches.

"This is ridiculous," complained Johnny. He crossed his arms and examined the birds in the trees.

"No fun!" cried Tommy, who sat down in the recently cut grass.

"You sure you're my age?" asked Vinnie, taunting Mike.

"All right. One more pitch," said Joe. He went into his pitching motion.

Mike focused his eyes on the ball. His mind locked on controlling his arms.

The pitch came in. Mike swung.

PLACK!

The yellow bat collided with the ball and sent it sailing toward Vinnie, who camped under the pop-up and caught it.

"Yeah Mike!" shouted Kristin. She ran up to him and patted his helmet. "If you didn't smack that pitch, I was going to have to take over for your brother. It wasn't the hitter. It was the pitcher that was the problem." Kristin wrinkled her nose at Joe, who understood she was being kind to Mike.

"Great job, little dude," said Johnny. "Finally."

A grin formed on Mike's face. He liked Wiffle ball.

Tommy ran over and took the bat from Mike. "Hey, you wanna sleep over at my house tonight?" he said to Joe.

"Sure," said Joe. "I'll ask my mom later." Joe turned to catch the ball that Vinnie had tossed his way.

"Can I come too?" asked Mike.

Tommy paused. "No. Um. I don't think my parents will let you."

Mike's heart sank. He knew right away it was because of his epilepsy—his friends' parents were always worried that Mike would have a seizure while they were watching him and they wouldn't know what to do about it.

"Oh!" said Joe, all of a sudden. "That's right. I have to stay home tonight; I forgot about this major math quiz on Monday." He and Mike casually looked at each other. Joe pitched the ball to Tommy, who smacked it over the third base line. Mike knew that Joe didn't have to stay home, but was fibbing because he was a great big brother who wanted to protect Mike's feelings.

Later that night, Mike's dad pulled up the covers as he tucked Mike in for bed. Mike jokingly kicked them down again. "Cut that out, Sport," his dad said, as he pulled the covers up again. He gently kissed his son's forehead.

Mike paused. "Dad?"

"Yes, son?"

"Since I always have my helmet on, I wish I could ride a bike. I could ride and no one would think twice about that dumb thing."

His dad chuckled and sat down beside Mike on the bed. "Big things are going to happen. Trust me."

Mike smiled as his dad gave him a high five. He knew he could trust anything his dad said. He thought about the feeling he had when his bat connected with the Wiffle ball, and how Kristin cheered him on—and he liked it. His dad turned the light off. As the room grew dark, Mike had a strange sensation that something special was about to happen to him.

Chapter 4

Love at First Bounce

The next day, Mike's dad had a great idea. He went to the local sporting goods store and purchased a brand new basketball. As soon as he came home, he shouted, "Mike!" Moments later, Mike came running into the kitchen. "I bought you something today," Mike's dad said, and held out the ball. Mike gazed at it, then up at his dad, who dribbled it once and bounce passed it to him.

Mike paused with the ball in his hands, not sure if a basketball was something he wanted. He bounced it once, then quickly looked at his mom. He could see from her eyes that it was OK. He bounced it twice. Then again. With every bounce of that ball Mike's smile grew bigger and bigger.

After a few minutes of dribbling, Mike and that basketball were like best friends. Something wonderful happened when *that ball* touched his hands. Mike had finally found something he could do!

"OK. Now dribble outside where you and that ball belong," said his mom.

Mike headed outside excitedly with his new ball. He dribbled it around his driveway. He dribbled it into the garage. He tried dribbling it on the grass, but that didn't work out so well. He dribbled it the entire rest of the day.

The next day, Mike dribbled it more, whenever he could.

Mike dribbled that basketball constantly, every day. Rain or shine, hot weather or cold—it didn't matter. He even dribbled while walking his dog, Sweetie. That basketball went with Mike everywhere. Even to bed.

The spring air blew gently through Mike's hair as he waited outside his school for the bus to pick him up. As always, his basketball was by his side. He dribbled it as he waited.

"Why d'you always have that ball with you?" It was Vinnie. He stood several feet away from Mike, as if Mike had some sort of contagious disease.

"Because I like it," said Mike.

"You're weird," Vinnie snorted. He shook his head and walked away.

"No, you're not," said Kristin, as she walked over to Mike. Kristin wore grey leggings and a t-shirt with an owl on it. "He's just jealous that the kids are talking about you."

"Kids are talking about me?" asked Mike, a bit worried.

"Yeah, but in a good way," Kristin reassured him. "Everyone's amazed by your dribbling. You're like a mini–Harlem Globetrotter."

Mike smiled.

"Here. Pass it." Kristin stuck her hands out for the ball.

Mike paused. The look on his face showed that he struggled with whether or not to share the ball. Then, he passed it behind his back. Kristin caught it and passed it back, the same way.

"Impressive," laughed Mike.

"I've got skills too." Kristin gave Mike a high five.

Mike placed the ball on the ground. He then punched it with his fist, causing it to slowly rise. With a few gentle taps, he started dribbling it. First inches from the ground, then higher and higher.

"Michael. Please. Stop bouncing that ball." It was Mrs. Barnes, the school principal. "It'll get away from you and in the street and the buses are coming." She walked up to him briskly. "I'll take that for a while." Mrs. Barnes grabbed the ball from Mike.

"Hey, that's mine," said Mike, trying not to be disrespectful with his tone.

"You can get it back another time," answered Mrs. Barnes. "Now pay attention. Your bus is coming."

A lump formed in Mike's throat. He tried to swallow it down as he felt himself want to cry. He fought back the tears.

"Please have your mother call me about it," said Mrs. Barnes.

"OK," Mike replied through the lump in his throat, as the bus pulled up.

"I can't believe she did that," whispered Kristin.

"Tell me about it," Mike sighed. "Nothing ever goes my way."

Mike and Kristin joined the other boys and girls in line and climbed on board the bus. He took a seat and Kristin sat next to him. Mike stared out the window at his ball in Mrs. Barnes's hands. His dad had given him that ball and he wanted it back.

When Mike got home, he quickly told his mom about what had happened. Mike and his mom drove back to school to meet with the principal and get his ball back. As they walked inside the building, Mike looked at the bench outside Principal Barnes's office and thought about all of the classmates he'd seen parked on it, waiting to go inside. *It's like the bench of doom*, Mike thought. He imagined himself as the principal and Mrs. Barnes waiting on that bench to go see him. He cracked a grin while his mother knocked on the door and was called in.

Mike had never seen the inside of Mrs. Barnes's office before. To him, it looked pretty normal and he couldn't understand why everyone was so afraid to go there.

Mike's mom and Principal Barnes exchanged pleasant hellos. Then the tone changed:

"I'm concerned about Michael," said Mrs. Barnes. "He's obsessed with this basketball. He's dribbling it everywhere—been doing so for weeks."

"Is he dribbling it during class?" asked Mike's mom.

"No," answered Mrs. Barnes.

"How about during lunchtime or at an assembly?" asked Mike's mom.

"No. Not to my knowledge," replied the principal.

"Then I don't see what the problem is," said Mike's mom. "If he's dribbling before school, at recess, and after school, there shouldn't be an issue."

"He should be doing other things with his time," started Mrs. Barnes.

"I'm OK with all the dribbling," Mike's mom cut in. "And if I'm OK with it, everyone else should be too." She smiled, and her tone was kind. "May we please have the ball back?"

Mrs. Barnes walked over to her couch, picked up the ball, and handed it to Mike.

Mike let the ball bounce, dribbled it once, then held it to his side. He looked up at his mom.

"Thank you," said Mike's mom to Principal Barnes. "We appreciate your concern."

"Yes, I was only trying to be helpful," replied Mrs. Barnes.

Mike's mom opened the door to leave. Mike waved goodbye to Principal Barnes, and he felt like he had the coolest mom on the planet. Mike dribbled the ball as he and his mom walked down the hallway. He knew that the ball was helping him develop coordination. In fact, he had just been switched from his special gym class into gym class with all the other boys and girls in his grade.

Team Doc

Mike's mom and dad loved to watch him play basketball on the driveway. Mike didn't have to wear a helmet anymore, because he had stopped having the "drop" seizures that made him fall down, thanks to medications he took. The medicines were like vitamins for Mike's brain. After hours of practice, Mike had become a very good dribbler and shooter. And he wanted to join his town's recreation basketball league for fourth graders. Yet, his parents worried about his epilepsy. Mike worried too, because he loved basketball more than anything and didn't want epilepsy to get in the way of playing.

Even though his medicine helped prevent Mike from having drop seizures, he still had more generalized, "tonic-clonic" seizures that caused him to black out, fall to the ground, and shake uncontrollably. This could happen if Mike was tired or didn't take his medication, but it could also happen for no reason at all. Mike often wondered what he looked like when he had a tonic-clonic seizure, because when they happened, he didn't even know. Seizures happen when the brain works differently than it normally does, and part of the different way the brain works keeps most people having seizures from realizing that they're having them. Mike found blacking out scary, and his mom worried because it can be dangerous.

Mike's mom thought he was old enough to see what happened to him during a seizure. She found a video at the library that showed someone having a tonic-clonic seizure like the ones he'd been having since the drop seizures stopped. Mike watched it. "I do that?" he asked.

"Yeah," answered his mom.

Mike realized why he was so exhausted after a seizure. He worried more. "What if that happens while I'm playing basketball?" he asked. "No one will want me playing, then."

"I think we both need to worry less about everything and have a talk with Dr. Karen," said his mom firmly.

A few days later, during his next doctor appointment, Mike and his parents asked a lot of questions. Dr. Karen told them that Mike would be safe playing basketball. Upon hearing that news, Mike wore the biggest smile of his entire life. The good news made him practically forget all about how chilly he was with his shirt off for the medical exam.

"Here are more of the cards I gave you for your school gym class," said Dr. Karen. "Your basketball team should find these helpful." She handed Mike special cards to give to his coaches and teammates—and anyone else who might need them.

The cards explained what to do if Mike should have a tonic-clonic seizure, which is the most common and recognizable kind of seizure. They did so using the word TRUST:

T: Turn the person having a seizure on his or her side.

R: Remove harmful objects from the area.

U: Use something soft under his or her head.

S: Stay calm.

T: Time the seizure. If the person has never had a seizure, or if the seizure lasts longer than five minutes, or if there are more than two seizures, call 911.

The card also informed the reader never to hold down a person having a seizure or put anything in his or her mouth. To do so could be harmful, and could even shatter the person's teeth because seizures involve uncontrollable movements and shaking.

"I hope a seizure never happens when I'm playing hoops or at school in front of all my friends," said Mike. "Everyone will make fun of me."

"It's wrong for anyone to make fun of you because of your epilepsy," said Dr. Karen. "Your *true* friends will stick by you no matter what. And if anyone makes fun of you, you should tell your teacher or parents."

Mike felt comfortable opening up and talking with his doctor. He shared that having epilepsy was really difficult, especially with all his schoolwork and the other pressures of being a kid.

"I'm scared," Mike said. "I've got so many dreams and goals, especially with basketball."

Dr. Karen smiled. "I'll tell you a secret. Even with epilepsy," she whispered, "you can do anything you set your mind to do. And playing basketball is great for your body. Go for it!"

Mike gave her a high five.

"I'd also like to suggest you meet with a psychologist or school counselor," added Dr. Karen. "It might be good to talk to someone else about your concerns and feelings. There are a few psychologists I can refer you to, or you can check with your school, too."

Mike's mom thought that was a terrific idea. She agreed to contact the school. Mike just listened.

They left the doctor's office, and Mike felt reassured that he had a good shot at going for his hoop dreams and living with epilepsy.

The next day, Mike's mom called his school and set up an appointment for them both to meet Dr. Garvey, his school counselor.

The idea of going talking to Dr. Garvey made Mike nervous. He didn't quite understand what she did. Mike's mom told him that school counselors and psychologists help kids understand their emotions. And that all he had to do was talk to her and share his experiences and what he was feeling. She also told him that counselors can help children with all kinds of worries, from being inse-cure because of weight problems to having trouble in school to being scared at night or sad because a loved one died. If you need help from a school counselor or psychologist it doesn't mean you're weird or dumb—it means you're smart because you made the good decision to see one.

As Mike walked down the hall toward the therapist's office, he remembered all his mom had told him. He still was a little jumpy inside. *What if she doesn't like me? Or know anything about epilepsy? What if the guys find out and make fun of me?* He looked up and down the hall to make sure no one saw as both he and his mom entered Dr. Garvey's office. Mike was glad he had his basket-ball with him. *I hope I'm allowed to take this in here*, he thought.

Mike and his mom approached Dr. Garvey's office.

"You must be Michael. How are you? I'm Dr. Garvey," the coun-selor said with a smile as she extended her hand to shake his.

"I'm fine," said Mike, although he felt like he was lying. The in-side of his stomach seemed like it held a thousand butterflies zoom-ing around and bumping into each other.

"Thanks for making the time to meet with us," said Mike's mom.

Mike glanced around at Dr. Garvey's office. He saw lots of toys on her shelves—Legos, stuffed animals, Hot Wheels cars, a harmon-ica, a kazoo, and even a gumball machine. There was also a small couch and her desk and chair.

Dr. Garvey asked Mike and his mom to sit down and be com-fortable. She told Mike that their meetings would remain private. She wouldn't even tell her husband. She did mention that there might be times when she may have to share what he said with his parents or teachers. Like if a fellow student treats him differently because of his epilepsy and she knows about it and thinks the situation might get dangerous, then she'll need to share that, so the school can help change that student's behavior. That doesn't mean she's being a tattletale or breaking her privacy rule. It just means there are certain times when she may have to share bits and pieces of information to keep everyone safe.

After a few minutes of listening to Dr. Garvey's voice and answering her questions, Mike began to feel comfortable. He could tell she really cared and he liked that. In fact, Mike needed that. Although he loved his mom, there were times he didn't want to tell her everything. He was glad he had someone else to talk to.

"Should I tell my friends I talk to you?" asked Mike. He wondered if he could trust Kristin not to tell or make fun of him. He knew he could.

"That's up to you," said Dr. Garvey. "Sometimes when kids don't understand something, they say mean things. So maybe just pick carefully who you tell."

Mike liked that advice.

"I meet with several boys and girls here, some in your grade, some older," said Dr. Garvey. "We talk about a lot of things. You're not the only one meeting with me."

Mike wondered who else sat on the same couch. He had a few ideas, but he kept himself from asking.

"I think this is great," said Mike's mom. "I'm glad his doctor recommended this."

Mike dribbled his ball. But as quickly as he started, he stopped. He realized that sound traveled and if anyone was there after school and heard a basketball bouncing, they'd know it was him inside. *I better leave this ball over there so I'm not tempted to dribble it,* he thought.

Mike showed Dr. Garvey the card his epilepsy doctor gave him to share with his basketball teammates and others at school.

"It's great that your doctor was able to give you those cards," said Dr. Garvey. "It's especially great that you feel OK about giving them to your teachers and coaches. Giving those cards is a little bit like giving everyone a short lesson about epilepsy. You're teaching them things they might not know. Do you think you'd feel more comfortable if your classmates knew more about epilepsy?"

"Yeah," said Mike.

"Tell you what…how about I work with you and we'll create a presentation you could give to the class?"

Mike paused. Giving people the cards was easy, but giving a presentation about epilepsy made him nervous. A thousand reasons why not to do it flooded his brain. Dr. Garvey noticed that Mike didn't jump on the idea.

"It's OK for you to have all the thoughts you have about your epilepsy," said Dr. Garvey. "There are no bad emotions. What matters is how you deal with the emotions you don't like. Through our talks we'll discover the best way to deal with whatever you are experiencing."

Mike smiled. "Can I get back to you on the presentation thing?"

"Sure," said Dr. Garvey. "And if you prefer to do it without me, that's fine too. Just know, you're not weak or crazy for seeing a therapist. You should be proud for taking this sometimes-scary step."

"Yeah, that's what Mom told me," Mike said, looking at her sitting next to him on the couch.

"We can discuss doing a presentation more tonight over dinner," said Mike's mom, who had been in listening mode to let Mike do the talking.

"Great," said Dr. Garvey. She looked at Mike. "I also want you to know that if you're ever bullied because of your epilepsy, don't respond to the bully, and always tell an adult, like a parent, teacher, or even me. OK? You wouldn't be tattling. And any adult you tell will be careful to take action that will address the bullying without getting you into trouble with the bully."

"I know that," said Mike. "Thanks." Mike began to fidget in his seat. Dr. Garvey knew this was the perfect time to finish their discussion. She thanked Mike and his mom for coming and they made arrangements for Mike to meet with her once a week for five or six weeks. Mike left her office feeling a lot better. He was glad that Dr. Garvey was on his team, even if he secretly thought she talked too much sometimes.

Chapter 6

The Perfect Outlet

The elementary school gymnasium buzzed with excitement as the boys took their warm-up shots for their first game. For many, it was the first game of the season. But for Mike, it was the first real basketball game of his life. Mike grinned as he dribbled for the layup drill. He looked at the other team and wondered how he'd ever get a shot off without being stuffed. The boys were much taller than him. Mike knew exactly how he would score—and it made his smile beam brighter.

Mike looked up at his parents in the stands. His father gave him the thumbs up. His mom smiled brightly.

Moments later, the game started. Mike's team lost the tip-off and the other team dished the ball downcourt. The shot went up. Mike placed himself under the basket and maneuvered his body for the rebound. But his bigger opponent easily boxed him out, jumped, and scored.

Mike took the pass from his teammate and dribbled down the court. His heart raced like an engine. For the first time in a long time, he felt like a normal kid. He blocked out his fears about having a seizure and focused his mind on the basketball hoop before him. *Time to show the team what I can do,* Mike thought to himself.

As Mike approached the half-court line, his defender came toward him. Mike was happy the other coach had his team playing man to man. Mike easily dribbled by his defender. He even included a behind-the-back dribble in his move. Within seconds he was open and took his shot, which went in the hoop.

In the stands, Mike's dad stood and clapped.

Mike ran back down the court. He could see from the looks on everyone's faces that his opponents and many parents were surprised he could dribble and score. *See, kids with epilepsy are just like everyone else,* he wanted to say. But he didn't have to—his dribbling and scoring said that for him.

Although Mike and his team played well, they were no match for the other team, which was made up of much taller boys. Even though Mike scored 21 points, his team lost.

"I hate this feeling," Mike said to his father, as he zipped up his warm-up jacket after the game.

"Get used to it. You can't win every game," replied his dad.

"I know," chirped Mike, pulling up his sweatpants over his team shorts.

"Great game!" It was Bobby, one of Mike's teammates. Bobby had bushy black eyebrows that were almost as curly as his hair.

Mike nodded. "Thanks," he added, with a smile. *I did play well today,* he thought. *I'm so glad...*

"I know what you're thinking," said his dad.

"You do?" asked Mike.

"You're thinking you're so glad Dr. Karen said you could play."

"Oh my gosh, you're right. I was just thinking that," said Mike.

"I know my son." Mike's dad smiled.

As Mike put his winter jacket on, he realized he hadn't thought or worried about having a seizure for most of the game. He liked the focus that basketball gave his mind, and how good his body felt exercising. And, for the first time in a long time, he liked himself.

Chapter 7

Hard Fouls

And so Mike kept on dribbling. He played basketball before school. At lunchtime. And every day after school, even past sundown. He still had seizures from time to time, but, so far, never on the court. And playing basketball made him happier and able to better deal with his different life.

Mike also kept taking his medications, typically three times each day. The medicine helped his seizures happen less frequently. Every time Mike took a pill, he'd say, "Vitamins for my brain," to himself. Mike had a special medication case that stayed with the school nurse. The case helped her know what medicine Mike needed to take and when. Mike often felt embarrassed going to the nurse's office, because none of the other kids in his class had to go there to get their medication. Sometimes, the nurse would even meet him in the lunch room with his medicine. Mike also made sure he got plenty of rest, ate healthy foods, and stayed active by playing basketball.

Before long, Mike dribbled circles around the other boys his age. When Mike was 12, no one could keep up with him—he was the best player on the playground. After hours of practice, Mike could also do amazing tricks with his basketball, like dribbling two balls at one time, blindfolded.

But as Mike grew up, in addition to having epilepsy, he was always the smallest guy on the team. "Why can't things be easier?" Mike asked his dad.

"Look at all you've accomplished so far," his dad responded. "Remember, I told you when you were little that big things will happen if you keep trying. You have to promise me that you'll continue to do your best and never give up."

Mike spun the ball on his finger. "I promise."

○ ○ ○

The fall air was crisp and invigorated Mike with a jolt of excitement and energy. During his walk home from school, he dribbled with one hand and carried his books in the other—it was his daily routine. As he strolled by driveway after driveway, each with a basketball hoop, he imagined himself dribbling down every one and scoring. In fact, it took all of Mike's strength to resist the temptation to do just that. Suddenly...

"Hey loser!"

It was Vinnie, who now was the biggest boy in Mike's grade.

"Why d'you love basketball so much?" Vinnie crossed the street and walked quickly toward him. Mike locked eyes with Vinnie, but kept walking. He even quickened his pace. A few seconds later, Vinnie appeared right in front of him. "Hey! You deaf and small?" Vinnie asked.

"No. Just small," replied Mike. "What's up?"

"The sky," sneered Vinnie. Just then, Vinnie's eyes froze on Mike's basketball. His hands darted like a striking snake and he took the basketball away from Mike's grip.

Mike paused. He exhaled a short burst of air. The official NBA leather ball was brand new, a gift from his mom. Mike's mind raced, thinking about how to get it back.

"What are you, a baby? Why do you play with this ball so much?" Vinnie said, admiring the ball.

"I don't know. I just do," said Mike. He thought about grabbing the ball back as fast as he could, but didn't want to provoke a fight.

In the background, other kids walking home from school had stopped to watch them, sensing a fight could happen at any moment. Mike looked up at Vinnie. Just as Mike was about to speak, Vinnie said, "This ball doesn't want to be dribbled any more. I think it wants to be kicked!"

Vinnie dropped the ball and booted it as hard as he could. The ball soared into the air. Each revolution seemed like it was in slow motion to Mike. He couldn't believe this was happening to him. He made sure he watched exactly where the ball landed, which was in the woods between two houses. Mike's heart sank then started to pulse like an engine. His hands twitched nervously.

"What are you going to do now, have *another* seizure or something?" snarled Vinnie.

"No," replied Mike. He clenched his fists at his side like a boxer. Vinnie noticed Mike's fingers curl to his palm.

"Go ahead. I dare you." Vinnie's eyes practically threw fireballs with each syllable that came out of his mouth.

Mike didn't flinch. He remembered his mother's advice about keeping calm when provoked to a fight. He took a deep breath, unclenched his hands, and glanced at his schoolmates, who were standing and watching nearby.

"You're not so dumb after all," said Vinnie.

Mike turned and jogged toward the woods between the two houses. He knew he wasn't running away from a fight but rather to his ball.

"You're such a loser, Mike! Always will be!" shouted Vinnie. He shook his head and laughed. He smiled at the onlookers who rolled their eyes at him and casually re-started their walks home, putting distance between themselves and Vinnie.

Mike could hear the sound of the fall leaves crunching beneath his feet as he slowed down and picked up his ball. He examined his special gift carefully. But there it was—a big, black scuffmark from Vinnie's shoe. Anger filled his heart. He quickly wiped the dirt off the ball, but no matter how hard he rubbed, the scuffmark would not come off. He looked back for Vinnie, wanting to go back and fight, but he knew that wasn't the right thing to do. So Mike took a few deep breaths and calmed himself. He held the ball by his side and resumed his walk home.

Mike surged through his front door with the speed and force of a penned bull bolting out of a chute. He dropped his books on the stairs and headed for the kitchen and the refrigerator. Cool air splashed his face as he opened the fridge and studied its contents. Just then, his brother Joe grabbed the handle and opened the door further.

"What are you doing? Jerk." Mike gently pushed his brother.

"What's your problem?" Joe looked his brother up and down. "You're the one acting like a jerk." He brushed Mike aside, reached in and took out the orange juice.

"Hey, I wanted that." Mike grabbed for it and the juice spilled.

"Look at what you did now. I'm not cleaning that up." Joe glanced down at the juice on the floor and saw Mike's feet walk briskly over the spill, then out of the room. "Get back here and clean this up!"

"No way!" bellowed Mike as he ran down the hall. Upstairs in his room, Mike lay on his bed and threw his basketball up in the air and caught it. Suddenly, there was a knock on the door. "Go away," called Mike.

His mom slowly opened the door and entered. "What's wrong, honey? Joe told me about the juice that spilled and said that you weren't yourself. Everything all right?"

Mike sat up on his bed. "No. Nothing's all right. Everything's horrible. I hate being different. I hate epilepsy. I hate Vinnie. And every day I'm always wondering if a seizure is going to happen to me.

I feel like I just can't win." Mike stared at his bedspread and the floor.

Mike's mom sat beside him and he told her about everything that had happened on the way home from school that day and how he felt about it all. She assured him that she knew him better than anyone and that, while he was really mad at Vinnie, she knew he didn't hate anyone. She explained how she worries about when and where a seizure might happen to him, too, and that she does so especially when he's not with her. "I learned that we can't dwell on our worry," she explained. "We just have to believe that everything will be all right." And she told him that speaking about his worries, like he was doing now with her, was one of the best things he could do to help make things feel and be better. "It's always best to share what you're feeling with those who love you and care about you the most," she reminded him. "Remember what Dr. Garvey said about bullies? Maybe you should talk to her about what happened."

Mike shook his head. "I don't know. If Vinnie finds out, he'll pummel me."

Mike wiped the tears from his face with his sleeve. Then he chuckled, knowing his mom never liked it when he did that, but she always understood.

Mike's mom put her arm around him for a hug, and a smile appeared on his face. He did feel better because he spoke with her. *Man, she's always right,* he thought, *and she does know me better than anyone.* He made up his mind right then and there that he would tell Dr. Garvey about Vinnie. His mom also reminded him that it's normal to be embarrassed or upset if kids didn't understand his epilepsy or love for basketball, and that he can work on not letting that frustrate him. Mike spun the ball on his finger to show her that he felt better.

"Maybe one of these days I'll be able to do that," she said.

"Only if you practice real hard," said Mike, finally smiling for the first time since the walk home. He looked at the scuffmark on the ball. He made a promise to himself that every time he noticed that mark on the ball he'd remember the day he didn't let Vinnie defeat or discourage him.

The next day, after school, Mike walked to Dr. Garvey's office. He had gone back and forth all morning about whether or not he wanted to tell her about the episode with Vinnie. But when he dreaded walking home from school—and the possibility of another run in with Vinnie—he knew he had to say something.

Dr. Garvey was happy to see him. Mike told her everything about the ball-kicking scene and he described how scared and small it made him feel. Dr. Garvey shared that she felt the best thing to do was to tell the school's principal about it.

"But what if he beats me up next time?" asked Mike.

"I don't think that will happen," said Dr. Garvey. "We'll make sure it doesn't."

Mike's heart beat faster and his palms grew sweaty just thinking about it. Mike agreed to trust her. As he picked up his basketball and said goodbye to Dr. Garvey, he wondered if he had done the right thing by saying something to her.

Chapter 8

Not a Tattletale

Two days later, Mike headed down the hallway for his math class. Suddenly, he noticed Vinnie walking toward him. His head was down and his pace was much slower than usual. Mike stopped and pretended to read a flyer tacked to a bulletin board on the wall. He had one eye on the board and the other on Vinnie. He watched Vinnie stop in front of Principal Barnes's office, then slowly walk in. *That Dr. Garvey moves fast,* thought Mike. *Oh no. I'm dead meat after school.* The bell rang, but Mike didn't seem to care. He walked by the principal's office and noticed that Vinnie hadn't closed the door all the way.

Mike didn't know what to do. He knew he had to go to class. In a few minutes he'd be late. But there was Vinnie in Principal Barnes's office. *What were they going to say?* Mike just had to know. Another teacher, Mr. Wehner, who taught science, walked briskly down the hall. His bald head shined even in the lightest light. *He's late for class, too,* Mike thought, *but not late 'cause he was combing his hair.* Mr. Wehner gave Mike a lingering look, as if to say "get to class." Mike plopped himself down on the principal's bench as though he were next in line. Mike couldn't hear a word, but he knew in a minute the halls would be quiet and he might be able to make out something. Mike felt like a spy.

Soon, classes began and you could hear a pin drop in the school, if anyone were to drop one. Mike knew he shouldn't be eavesdropping but he couldn't help himself.

"But you did bully him, and it needs to stop," said Principal Barnes. Her voice was warm and friendly, but it carried a point. "The teachers and adults at school will be watching you closely and they won't turn a blind eye to any aggressive actions. Every adult at this school is committed to creating a safe environment for everyone to grow, socially and academically, without being afraid."

Wow, thought Mike. *She is good. No wonder no one ever wants to sit on this bench.*

"I can't believe he told on me. What a tattletale," said Vinnie.

Oh no. I'm dead. Mike wondered how much a bodyguard would cost.

"There's a difference between tattling and getting help when you feel like you or someone you know is in danger," said the principal. "Mike felt threatened by what you did and did exactly the right thing by talking to an adult about it. Just like if you ever feel threatened by anyone you should talk to an adult too."

Who'd threaten that beast? thought Mike. He couldn't believe how nice the principal's voice sounded. And he wished his mom and dad could always talk to him like that when he got in trouble.

"I will have to tell your parents about this Vinnie."

"Oh man. Please no," pleaded Vinnie.

"There's a special session I'd like you to attend during your recess time, too, for a while. Once a week."

"I'm going to miss recess?" Vinnie whined.

Oh man. I'm really dead. Mike wondered what other school he could transfer to. *Maybe dad could move to Alaska. They play basketball there. Although it's slippery and cold. Hawaii hoops would be better.*

"Did you know that Mike doesn't have it easy?" said the principal, changing the focus. "He has epilepsy."

"I know," said Vinnie. "He lives on my block. Across the street."

"It's not easy for Mike having epilepsy," repeated the principal. A pause.

"I've seen him have seizures before. From my house."

"And how did that make you feel?" asked Principal Barnes.

"I don't know. It was weird."

"Scary weird?"

"Yeah, kind of."

"Imagine how it makes Mike feel. You know, he doesn't ever know when it might happen. And when it happens he doesn't know it's happening. He's in a blackout. It's something he has to live with every day. That's why he needs *friends*, not someone mistreating him."

Another pause.

"If you live on the same block, why can't you be friends?"

"I dunno," blurted Vinnie. He pondered for a moment, then explained, "We just never clicked. You can't be friends with everyone."

Principal Barnes smiled at Vinnie. "True, but we can be friendly."

Does she actually think we can be friends? wondered Mike.

"Can I go now?" asked Vinnie. Mike could practically hear the bully's eyes rolling.

Mike stood up and planned his exit route should the conversation end and Vinnie be out in the hallway with him. He did not want to be planted on the bench when that happened.

"Listen, Vinnie. You're a great kid. Just know that Mike didn't ask for me to talk to you. He doesn't even know we're having this conversation."

Wrong.

"Put yourself in his shoes for a while. Think about what it might be like to be him, and to be him with you in his life. He's a nice boy too, and a pretty good basketball player."

And she hasn't even seen me play, thought Mike, still standing, ready to dart away at a moment's notice. Mike knew at any moment his math teacher could send somebody down the hall to look for him.

"I know. Why's he so special?" said Vinnie. "Getting so much attention..."

"Everyone in this school is special, including you," replied the principal. "We have lots of kids that need special attention because of things going on in their lives. Some of it is not so nice."

"You should go watch Mike play basketball sometime. And remember: Think about what it's like to be in his shoes. And yes, you can go now." Principal Barnes stood up. "I'll let you know about those special sessions."

Mike looked right. He bolted like he was on a sudden, fast break and made a right turn around the corner and out of sight. He scuttled into the boys' bathroom and waited behind the door, hoping that Vinnie went left instead of right. He paused a few moments and when he felt the coast was clear, slowly opened the door and tentatively peered ahead down the hall. He stepped outside. As he expected, Melissa, a cute girl with frizzy red hair and glasses, was coming from his math class right towards him.

Mike was thrilled she'd seen him come out of the bathroom. He had his excuse and he knew his math teacher would never reprimand him for being in the bathroom, which was true enough for Mike to share. He had been in there, after all.

Chapter 9

Bankable Shot

No matter how much Mike tried to turn the channel on his thoughts he just could not do it. He tried to think about his favorite basketball moves. Or his favorite basketball player. Or Kristin. Or ice cream. Or his favorite TV show, *Bugs Bunny*. Or his mom. Or the beach, or playing hoops on the beach, or even something goofy like fierce ninja monkeys. Nothing worked. His thoughts still came back to Vinnie. Mike tried to look like he was paying attention as his math teacher, Mr. Myron, a skinny man with a bow tie and plaid jacket, wrote on the smart board. But it was all an act. Mike replayed every word of the conversation he had just heard in his mind. The only thing he calculated was how long it would take for Vinnie to find him and do more than kick the snot out of his basketball. The answer didn't please him.

Mike coughed out a soft, nervous laugh and glanced over at Kristin, who was looking attentive. She made eye contact with him and his eyes begged for her to talk to him. As soon as the bell rang, Kristin waited in the hall for Mike. "You're not gonna believe what happened," he said. Mike shared everything with Kristin, as quietly and quickly as he could, while they walked to their lockers. "You can't leave me," he said, knowing lunch and recess were next, and that would be an opportunity for Vinnie to see him. *And pound me.*

"I shoot baskets with you every day," said Kristin. "Why would today be any different?"

"I don't know. With my luck, you'd have scheduled lunch with some movie star or something today of all days." He opened his locker and took out his basketball. He paused. "Maybe we should skip lunch and go to the library today?"

"We'll do no such thing," said Kristin, in a perfect imitation of Mike's mom. She broke character to say, "I'll be with you, OK? Nothing bad will happen."

"You know, if I were bigger, I wouldn't need you to be there at all."

"Thanks a lot," said Kristin. "If you were bigger you wouldn't be in this position." Kristin hesitated. "I take that back. You still would be."

Mike and Kristin ate their lunch together near the back of the cafeteria. Mike noticed Vinnie look over at them out of the corner of his eye. His heart skipped a beat and his grape juice almost snorted out of his nose, but he tried to look cool, calm, and collected. Kristen and Mike made their way to the playground and found an unused basketball hoop to practice their shots. Mike loved how shooting gave his mind a focus that nothing else quite did.

"Don't look, but he's watching us," whispered Kristin, as she banked a shot. The bank shot was her best shot. She rarely missed.

Mike grabbed the rebound, passed the ball to her behind his back, and casually caught eyes with Vinnie. *Hmm. He doesn't look like he wants to pummel me,* thought Mike. *But neither does a lion before it pounces on its prey.*

Kristin and Mike kept shooting. Vinnie watched for a few minutes from across the paved parking lot, and then joined some of his friends passing a football. "Will you walk home from school with me today?" Mike asked Kristin.

Kristin chuckled. "Of course." She tried spinning the ball on her finger but it spun out of control.

Chapter 10

The Bathroom

The days seemed to move slower for Mike after he heard Vinnie talking to Principal Barnes. He wondered if Vinnie was trying to mentally torture him. A few weeks had gone by. Vinnie never said a word to him, but Mike noticed Vinnie watch him at lunch or in the hall or at recess. When they would catch each other's eye, Mike did his best to share a half smile. He even mustered up the courage to wave to him once.

Mike thought about Vinnie often. He even tried to do what Principal Barnes suggested Vinnie do about him—imagine himself in Vinnie's shoes. He wondered what it might feel like living across the street from a kid who had epilepsy and seeing him have seizures. And what it'd feel like to be the biggest kid in the grade. *I wish I knew what that felt like,* thought Mike. *It'd be neat to be tall for a day.* Mike knew that Vinnie's parents got divorced in the third grade and his mom had remarried. He realized it probably wasn't easy being Vinnie either.

Then, one day, the inevitable happened, just as Mike opened up the door to leave the boy's bathroom. There was Vinnie.

"Um. Hi," said Mike.

Vinnie paused. His face revealed that he didn't know what to say, either.

"I'm ahhh...sorry...that you...have to miss recess once a week," said Mike. *Why did I say that? Think. Recover.* "That stinks. I have to miss recess sometimes for doctor's appointments. It's the worst."

"How did you know about that?" asked Vinnie, still holding the door open.

"Well because…it's because of me," mumbled Mike. "I never meant to get you in trouble. I was just feeling scared and didn't know what to do, and the adults sort of took over."

"Oh," said Vinnie.

There was an awkward pause.

"Can you move?" asked Vinnie. "I really have to go to the bathroom."

"Oh sure," said Mike, as he moved outside but held the door for Vinnie. "Um…have a great pee." The door closed and Mike hit himself on his own head with his hand. *Who has a great pee? I'm such a knucklehead. But at least I still have my head.* Mike was glad that conversation happened outside the bathroom and not inside, where it would have been even more uncomfortable.

Chapter 11

The Big Question

"You ready for tryouts?" It was Kristin, and she asked the question right after Mike had missed his first jump shot at recess.

"Based on that shot: no," said Mike. He had just told Kristin about his bathroom moment with Vinnie, and his concentration was off. He glanced back at the spot where he often saw Vinnie watching him and noticed Vinnie wasn't sitting there. He was walking towards him.

Oh no.

He motioned with his eyes. Kristin had no clue what he was trying to do.

"What's your problem?" she asked. "You look like you have to sneeze or something."

"Can I shoot?" It was Vinnie.

Kristin turned and her eyes got wide.

"Um. Sure," she said, and she bounce-passed the ball to him.

Mike didn't know if he should cringe or not. The last time Vinnie had held his ball he booted it like a European soccer star. Vinnie simply shot the ball, which hit nothing but net.

Mike grabbed the rebound.

"I noticed you weren't at recess yesterday," said Kristin to Vinnie, trying to make conversation.

Knowing where Vinnie had been, Mike winced, but Kristin didn't notice. "There's no law saying you have to come out for recess every day," said Mike. "You were probably catching up on homework or something." He bounce-passed the ball to Vinnie.

"Um, yeah. I had some stuff I *had* to do." Vinnie threw Mike a look that showed he was grateful that Mike kept his secret, and then he shot the ball again, but missed.

Kristin jumped in and got the rebound over Mike.

"Hey, no fair, you overgrown female," teased Mike.

"Almost all the girls are bigger than the boys in our grade," stated Kristin matter-of-factly, and she dribbled the ball to the top of the key.

"Not quite all the boys," said Vinnie.

Mike laughed. So did Kristin.

"You trying out for the travel team?" asked Kristin.

"Actually I am," said Vinnie.

There was silence as Mike and Vinnie looked at each other. Mike didn't know how to react to that news. His first instinct was not to be happy about it, but he made sure his face didn't reveal that.

"That's great," said Mike.

"I heard you're trying out." Vinnie motioned for Mike to pass him the ball. Mike did. Vinnie shot and scored.

"I am." Mike boxed out Kristin and got the rebound. He glanced to the right and noticed a few teachers with a watchful eye on him and Vinnie.

"Well at least you two won't be fighting for the same position," chuckled Kristin.

"You're not a point guard?" asked Mike, jokingly.

"Center," said Vinnie. "I wish I could dribble like you."

"Well, Mikey can show you a few tricks," said Kristin.

Mike rolled his eyes at the nickname, and wanted to ask her if she was crazy. Just having Vinnie there was making him feel nervous, although he seemed to grow more comfortable as the minutes passed. "Sure. Um...I can show you a few things. Watch this." Mike dribbled the ball between his legs, then behind his back. He even closed his eyes and did the same tricks. He realized that was probably too advanced to teach Vinnie right away so he showed him a simple drill to practice at home involving crouching on one knee and dribbling the ball around your body and through one leg.

Vinnie grinned as he watched Mike. When he tried to copy him, the ball scooted away. Vinnie quickly refocused, tried again, and did it.

"Atta boy," said Mike, sounding like his father.

Vinnie popped up on both legs and passed the ball to Mike. Just then, the playground volunteer blew her whistle, signaling the end of recess. Vinnie nodded at Mike and Kristin and jogged away.

"What just happened?" asked Kristin.

Mike shrugged.

Full Court Press

B alls of sweat beaded on the foreheads of all the boys running up and down the basketball court. Mike dribbled expertly past the boy defending him and launched his shot.

Swish!

Coach Parker smiled as he watched his shortest player score easily.

Mike wiped the sweat off his hands across the letters on his travel team jersey. The coach had seen Mike play in the recreational league and suggested he try out. Just being asked had made Mike's day. But when Mike received the letter that he had made the team, he felt more proud than he had ever felt before. His mom framed the letter and hung it in Mike's room.

Mike's team, Allendale, was playing against one of their biggest rivals—Wyckoff. Allendale hadn't beaten Wyckoff in three years and Mike had made up his mind that he was going to help stop that losing streak. Vinnie had also made the team. His size and strength made the coaches' eyes light up. Vinnie received the same letter that Mike had, and when he came over one day after practice and saw Mike's framed, he asked his own mom to frame his as well.

"He dribbles like a Harlem Globetrotter," said one Wyckoff boy, observing Mike display his fancy dribbling skills. Mike dribbled behind his back, between his legs, and executed perfect cross-over dribbles as if he could do them in his sleep during the entire first quarter of the game. Being an expert dribbler helped Mike compensate for his short stature. He could get around and past his defenders and make himself open for a shot. He had scored 10 of his team's 16 points and they led Wyckoff by 2. Mike banked another shot in, putting his team up by four. He beamed as he jogged downcourt with his teammates. Vinnie gave him a low five.

As he turned to ready himself to play defense, Mike's body suddenly collapsed to the floor and shook forcefully.

Coach Parker's eyes widened in shock as he and all the other boys and assistant coaches raced to Mike. "Everyone stay back!" Coach Parker shouted, remembering the advice on the epilepsy card Mike had provided.

The assistant coach looked at her watch in order to time the seizure. There was nothing hard or sharp near Mike's head. That was good.

A look of fear and concern appeared on the faces of all of the players. No one knew what to do.

"Is he gonna be all right?" asked Vinnie.

"He'll be all right," said Mike's dad, approaching the court. "Just give him some space. This should end soon."

They watched Mike's legs, arms, and body twitch and flail.

A few minutes later, Mike's body stopped shaking. The seizure had ended. For everyone in the room, it had seemed like the longest three minutes of their lives.

Mike slowly regained control of his body. He had also blacked out and couldn't remember the past few minutes. But he knew what had taken place. He leaned up on his elbow and glanced at his fellow basketball players. He could only glimpse at them, not wanting them to see the embarrassment in his eyes. He couldn't act as if *nothing* had just transpired. He knew what they saw probably upset them, even scared them, and that they didn't understand.

"You all right?" asked a teammate, compassionately.

"I'll be fine," replied Mike, as his coach grabbed his arm, helping him get to his feet. The gym that had been full of the playful sounds of sneaker squeaks, grunts, running, and dribbling was now practically silent.

Mike rose to his feet. The parents on both sides of the gym applauded. Coach Parker escorted him off the court to his father. "Resume the game," said the coach to the referee. Mike finally made eye contact with his coach and wondered what he was thinking.

Mike rested on the sidelines next to his dad. The two watched Mike's team lose, again. After the game, Coach Parker told Mike that he wanted to talk to his father alone.

"I'm not sure it's such a good idea to have Mike on the team," said Coach Parker.

Mike's father couldn't believe what he had just heard. "Why? Is he suddenly not good enough?"

"No," replied the coach. "You know as well as I do that I can't have him playing if he's going to have seizures. It's not fair to the other players."

Mike's father's face started to turn as red as an apple.

"Plus, it's not safe. I can't risk it," said Coach Parker.

"Risk what?" asked Mike's dad. "Losing the game? Feeling embarrassed?"

Mike looked at his dad. He thought his dad was going to lose it. *Great, just what I need. I wish epilepsy had never come into my life,* he thought.

Vinnie walked up to Mike. "What's going on?"

"Coach doesn't want me on the team anymore."

"What?" said Vinnie. "That's not fair."

Mike's father composed himself. "Excluding Mike because of his epilepsy would be wrong. Plain and simple. Mike is no threat to the safety of the other players. Seizures can happen without notice and lots of people with epilepsy play sports and work at jobs throughout the world, every day.

"And anyway, Mike loves basketball," finished Mike's dad. "To keep him from playing would break his heart and send the wrong message to a young boy trying his very best. Not to mention what it would say to his teammates."

"I hear you. I just...I'm not sure," said Coach Parker.

"Look, I'm not worried about my son. His doctor isn't worried and neither is Mike. He should be on your team. And anyway, have you ever had such a good ball handler who can also shoot?"

"If Mike can't be on the team, then I won't be either." It was Vinnie. The rest of the team was standing behind him.

"Us too," said the other players, practically in unison.

Coach Parker paused for a moment, taking it all in. "OK...OK... um...I see. I'll give him a shot. He can stay on the team," he said. A half smile formed on his face and he extended his right hand for Mike's dad. They shook hands. Coach shook Mike's hand too.

Mike looked at his teammates. They could see the emotional and physical exhaustion he was feeling just from looking at his face. Having a seizure made Mike feel like he had just been through a heavyweight title fight. His eyes said thank you to his teammates, for standing up for him.

All during school the next day, Mike worried about what would happen if he had another seizure during a game or practice. His teammates had handled his first seizure well, with grace, even. *What if it happens again? Or keeps happening? Coach wouldn't put up with that. Maybe having that epilepsy card wasn't enough for Coach,* thought Mike.

At practice the next day, as the coach addressed the team, a small smile appeared on Mike's face. What if he talked to his team about epilepsy? Mike did owe Dr. Garvey an answer on whether he'd give an epilepsy presentation to his class and he figured talking to his team would work and would help everyone, even Coach Parker, understand better.

"Mike, what are you smiling about?" asked Coach. "Wait a sec... do you feel okay?"

"I feel great, Coach. You know, we have a plan for each game, so I think we should have a plan in case I have another seizure," explained Mike.

Coach Parker asked, "What do you suggest, Mike?"

"Maybe we can have assignments," said Mike. "Maybe one person is responsible for making sure there's nothing around me that could hurt me."

"Like boxing out someone. Only chairs, people, or sharp objects, instead," nodded Ahmad Patel, the team's forward. "I can do that."

"And somebody else can time me. If the seizure lasts more than five minutes, we need to call for help." Mike's voice was more confident.

"I have the stopwatch always, so I'll grab that assignment," said Coach Parker.

"If it happens during a practice or if my parents aren't here, someone will need to call them."

"I can do that," said Vinnie.

"Oh, and if possible, I'll need something soft under my head."

"Like Coach's belly," Vinnie joked. The team laughed.

"I see you wanna ride the bench, young man," said Coach Parker. "I'll have you know this is fun fat."

"I don't have any of that," laughed Vinnie.

"You don't have any fun," said the coach. He paused. "Jonesy, you can be responsible for making sure Mike gets a sweatshirt or something soft under his head if a seizure happens."

"Nothing too sweaty!" added Mike.

Coach Parker smiled. "A few last points on this topic. Was anyone scared the other day when the seizure happened to Mike?"

Mike glanced around the room. He could tell the guys were nervous about answering. Bobby Jones, who they all called Jonesy, raised his hand. "I was," he said.

"Me too," agreed Ahmad. "Practically all my life I've heard about epilepsy, but I'd never seen it before."

Vinnie nodded. "I've seen Mike have a seizure before, because we live near each other, but it's still scary to watch."

"I have to admit, I was a little scared too," said the coach. "And that's OK. From what I understand, it's pretty normal to be afraid of what we don't know. I think now we know that we can all handle this if it happens again. And I'm glad we have the plan. I think we'll all agree our job is much easier than Mike's. He has to live with this."

The boys nodded in agreement.

"Any of you have any questions for Mike?"

Vinnie raised his hand. "Yeah...what's it feel like when that's happening to you?"

Mike looked down at the ground. "Um...I don't realize it's happening. That's called blacking out. When it's over, I'm exhausted. I feel like I was just beaten up by a 300-pound gorilla." Mike looked up at his teammates. There was a long pause.

"Any other questions?" asked the coach.

No hands went into the air.

"Great. I'm glad we took the time to do this today, and I'm sure we all agree that we are glad Mike's on the team. He deserves to be here. Now, let's get out there and play some ball."

A few boys patted Mike on the back before they ran onto the court. At that moment Mike knew that there was something he loved even more than playing basketball: being part of a team.

Chapter 13

Birth of a Nickname

Three weeks later, Mike's team had made the county championship. Mike placed his basketball jersey over his head and pulled it down over his chest. *What if my shot's not on today?* He tucked his shirt inside his shorts. *What if I stink? Please no seizures.* Mike sat on his bed and started putting on his sneakers. *What if...?* He caught himself thinking unhelpful thoughts. He remembered a trick his dad had taught him, to imagine himself turning the channel, like on a TV set, on unhelpful thoughts and switching to positive ones. Mike pictured a TV set in his mind and remembered all the words of encouragement he'd received from his parents and doctors through the years. Old words of encouragement washed over him. *I can do this*, he thought. *I can't give up. I have to keep thinking positively. It will all work out.* Almost supernaturally, the butterflies in his belly disappeared—although he knew it wasn't really magic, but his TV trick, that did it.

Mike quickly tied his high-top sneakers, and then looked at his reflection in the mirror. He gave himself a wink and a nod. Then, he ran downstairs for breakfast, ready for the biggest game of his life.

Coach Parker had asked the boys to be at the gym an hour early instead of the usual 30 minutes. Mike had figured it was to get in some extra practice. The entire team was soon amazed to discover that the real reason for the extra time was a special guest at their game that day: "Too Tall" Randolph, a famous NBA player and a personal friend of Coach Parker's.

All the players were so surprised that their chins practically hit the floor as Too Tall jogged into the gym. He looked like a skyscraper wearing sweatpants and high tops.

The butterflies started to do the samba in Mike's stomach again. Having an NBA player watch him play felt like too much pressure.

"It's a pleasure to be here with you today," said Too Tall. "Are you dudes ready to have a good time?"

The boys cheered.

"To make it to the NBA, you have to be smart and you can never give up," said Too Tall. He had the boys' complete attention, especially Mike's. He spoke for a few minutes about the importance of being a team player instead of an individual standout or hotshot. Then, he taught the group a few drills. "Now let's see how well you guys paid attention. I need a volunteer." Hands shot up like rockets. He searched the team and locked eyes with Mike. "You. Come on out here."

Mike bolted up and onto the court.

"Now, let's see you do what I just did," said Too Tall, with a friendly but challenging tone.

Mike received his pass, looked at the hoop and envisioned the drill in his mind. Then, he jolted into action. Mike dribbled between the cones as if the ball were a natural part of his body. He stopped, spun, and launched his shot, which hit nothing but net.

A few claps developed into a loud applause.

Mike turned and jokingly bowed. He rebounded his ball. Just then, he had an idea. He quickly picked up another ball on the court and dribbled them both simultaneously back toward Too Tall Randolph, just as he had done hundreds of times in his driveway. Then, he shut both of his eyes tight and kept on dribbling. He spun and continued dribbling both balls.

"Now that, men, is a basketball player," said Too Tall, approvingly.

Mike knew he was showing off a bit, but he didn't care. He

wanted to prove to everyone that he had special skills. Talents even they didn't possess. He spun the ball on his finger for a few seconds, then let it drop to his knee and he knee-passed the ball to Too Tall.

"If he were any taller, I might just be worried about my job," said Too Tall. "Although I'm not sure he really listened to that part about not being a show-off," he joked.

The boys laughed.

Mike sat down and received plenty of low fives from his teammates. In his heart he felt nine feet tall.

"What's your name?" asked Too Tall.

"Mike."

"You remind me of Mighty Mouse," said Too Tall. "I'm going to call you Mighty Mike."

Mike beamed. He liked that name. No one had ever compared him to a superhero before—even a superhero that resembled a mouse.

"Good luck in your game today, boys," added Too Tall. "Play smart and with heart and you'll win." Too Tall nodded at Coach Parker and jogged off the court.

"Thank you, Fred," said Coach Parker.

"Fred?" said the boys. A few chuckled out loud. Too Tall met their eyes and the players stopped laughing immediately.

"Yes. Fred," sighed Too Tall. "Now you know my real name. But you can call me Too Tall...if you like to live," he added, jokingly. He gave Coach Parker a sarcastic "gee thanks" look, walked off the court, and took a seat in the stands. He sat next to a few parents who shook his huge hand and thanked him for talking to their team.

Mike looked at his dad, who used hand gestures to communicate with Mike about how amazingly tall Too Tall was. Mike mouthed the words, "I know."

"Boys, this is the biggest game of our season. You earned this and, win or lose, you have a lot to be proud of," said the coach. Just then, the other team entered the gymnasium.

Vinnie growled softly as he noticed their maroon and white warm up suits that said "Ridgewood" on the back.

"Easy, big fella," laughed Mike.

Mike began to smile as he noticed Dr. Karen enter the gym and sit by his father. Dr. Garvey was there too, sitting next to his mom. His brother Joe also climbed up the stands with Kristin. *She looks cute today,* thought Mike. Then he quickly changed the channel on that thought. Mike waved to everyone and ran onto the court for warm-up drills with the team.

"Yo, Mighty Mike!" said Too Tall with a grin.

Mike nodded back at him and laughed as he dribbled down for his layup. *I can't believe Too Tall Randolph knows my name. Please don't let me have a seizure today. Please let me play well.* Mike knew plenty of players in sports history had cracked under the pressure of big games, or even the pressure of having girlfriends or boyfriends or other people they loved watching them play. *I don't wanna be one of them.* Mike wiped the sweat from his palms onto his shorts.

Coach Parker huddled the team. He called out his starting five and they jogged onto center court. There was:

Mike, the point guard;

Jonesy, the other guard;

Vinnie, the center;

Ahmad Patel, the power forward; and

Aaron Bramble, the shooting forward.

The boys took their positions. The ref tossed the ball up for the tip-off and the game started.

In the stands, Mike's brother Joe softly called a play-by-play into a pretend microphone, which was really just his hand. "And this contest has begun, ladies and gentlemen, and it should be a great one. Allendale wins the tip. The ball is passed down court to Mike. He turns. Low post. High arching shot...and connects!"

Joe's mom turned to him. "You gonna do that the entire game?" she asked.

"You bet," said Joe.

Mike's mom shook her head. "You're weird. I love ya, but you're totally weird."

Joe did the play-by-play for every second of the game. He even told his pretend audience what the parents in the stands snacked on during time-outs and commented on their fashion mistakes. The Ridgewood Maroons battled the Allendale team. When one team was up by four, the other team would soon tie, and then be ahead. The score went back and forth for all four quarters. The only thing more tired than the boys doing the battling on the court was Joe's voice.

"We're still tied here in the fourth quarter with two minutes to go," said Joe. "Ridgewood in-bounds the ball. They pass it to the skinny guy who dishes to tall guy...someone needs to check that kid's birth certificate. It looks like he shaves....The ball ends up in the hands of the bigger guy. The fade away! Got it! Who would have thought that kid could make that shot? And Ridgewood takes the lead." Joe turned to Kristin. "What are your thoughts?"

"I'm wishing you had laryngitis," she said.

Joe's mom laughed. "I'll second that."

Joe ignored his critics and talked into his fist. "One minute forty seconds left. Jonesy inbounds the ball to Mike. He dishes to Bramble....Inside for the shot and SCORE! Allendale chips away the score once again to tie this up."

The parents and fans around Joe all stood and cheered.

"One minute twenty remaining. Ridgewood rushes the rock down the court. Skinny guy again. He shows perimeter range. It's a scary shot. He wants a three....He got it! Now Allendale is down by three, with a minute and fifteen remaining."

"Teamwork guys! We can do this!" shouted Vinnie.

"And there's the pass to little Mike Simmel. Here's a guy who scored 18 points today. The pass to Jonesy. Shoots, misses. Offensive rebound Bramble. No good! And the fast break Ridgewood. It's a three on one. In for two! And now Allendale trails by five. With 50 seconds remaining."

"You're making me more nervous with all that commentary," said Mike's mom.

"Maybe some peanut butter would make him stop talking," suggested Kristin.

"I know. Isn't this great?" Joe turned his attention back to the game, totally oblivious to the fact that his response hadn't made sense.

"And it looks like Coach Parker has replaced Vinnie Bavagnoli, the Italian Stallion, with Lloyd Syvertsen....There's little Mike bringing the ball down again. Let's hope he doesn't blow this one."

Kristin elbowed Joe.

"He drives, spins...oh, what a beautiful behind-the-back pass to Jonesy...who dishes to Lucky Lloyd Syvertsen....The shot....Swish baby! And we're...I mean, Allendale trails by three! Good decision Coach Parker....Ridgewood inbounds the ball and there's the press by Allendale. Aaron B. steals the ball, shoots, and scores! This is now a 1-point game with 20 seconds remaining. Ridgewood calls a time out."

Coach Parker diagrammed what he wanted his players to do. The whistle blew and both teams took their positions. Mike's heart felt like it would burst from his chest. *Do I pass or shoot? What should I do if I get the ball?* He didn't have the answer.

"Go Mighty Mike!" yelled Vinnie from the sidelines.

"Yeah, get the ball to Mighty Mike!" shouted Too Tall from his seat.

"We gotta get the ball first," called Coach Parker.

Suddenly, Mike felt a little woozy inside. He tried to change the channel and refocus on the game.

"And the ball is in play for Ridgewood," muttered Joe. "The pass...and there's the steal by Jonesy! He dishes to Mike..."

"Might-tee Mike! Might-tee Mike!" chanted the boys on Mike's team. Mike passed the ball to Aaron. "Allen-dale! Allen-dale!" he shouted.

Suddenly, Mike took the pass back from his teammate. Instinctively, he raced the ball toward the hoop. Within seconds his defender guarded him tightly. Mike faked right, spun as he dribbled between his legs, and left his defender in his wake. Suddenly, another guard covered him like a glove.

He knew his team was down by one point. The clock counted down, and the crowd shouted, "10, 9, 8..."

Mike froze for a moment. *You've come a long way, dude,* he thought to himself.

Mike waited as Lloyd picked his defender. He dribbled by him and dished the ball to Ahmad who cut to the hoop. Seconds later, the ball had made its way back into Mike's hands. He stopped and froze.

"Three! Two!" yelled the crowd...

Mike popped his shot.

Swish!

The horn sounded.

"Game over! Mighty Mike sinks the shot! Allendale wins!" Joe stood on his feet and kissed his hand. "Way to go little brother!"

"You need help," said Kristin, rolling her eyes at Joe, but smiling to show she was kidding.

On the court while his teammates were whooping and jumping and celebrating, Mike smiled shyly. No one would have guessed that he just made the game-winning shot. Mike made his way to the sideline.

"You never give up do you?" said Coach Parker.

"Nope. Gotta give it your all and not be afraid to fall," said Mike. "Learned that a while ago."

"Great game, Mike," said Coach.

"I'm glad he's so short," said Too Tall, loud enough to generate a laugh from the crowd. "My job's safe!"

Mike's mom and dad hugged. Joe was still calling the play-by-play as Kristin rolled her eyes.

Mike looked at Dr. Karen and Dr. Garvey and mouthed the words "Thank you." The counselor winked back at him.

Vinnie, Ahmad, Aaron and Jonesy crowded around Mike. His teammates smothered him in a happy dog-pile. Suddenly, Mike felt his body rise into the air as Vinnie held him up like a trophy. "Mighty Mike nothing," Vinnie said, jokingly. "I'm the mighty one."

Mike's teammates jumped up and down in celebration chanting "Might-tee Mike! Might-tee Mike!"

Mighty Mike, thought Mike, happily. *I like the sound of that.*

— THE END —

A Note From Mighty Mike

Hi. I'm Mighty Mike. The real Mighty Mike. I'm a lot like the Mighty Mike character you just read about. In fact, his story is based on my experience growing up with epilepsy, overcoming obstacles, and believing that everyone has a chance to be successful. *Mighty Mike Bounces Back* is an example of one kid who learns from his experiences.

Like the Mighty Mike in the story, I once had a major epileptic seizure at a basketball camp. I was 16, and my family and I refused to let the camp send me home. Obstacles like that one made me stronger. As a teenager, my seizures came back and continued right through my adult years. Currently, I continue to take medication for my epilepsy and follow a physician's care. It's important for everyone, but especially people with epilepsy, to take care of their bodies, get the necessary sleep, handle adversity with patience, and communicate honestly and openly with others.

I continued to work hard to develop my basketball skills, and I kept thinking positively and changing the channel on unhelpful doubts, worries, and fears. I also got creative and developed more and more tricks that I could do with a basketball. I was captain of my college basketball team, graduated from college, and, while I was never invited to play for an NBA team, I did get another special opportunity. During a tryout, I impressed the owner of the famous Harlem Wizards, and now I'm a member of a professional entertainment basketball team.

I'm also a one-man show, performing at special events and college and NBA half-times. And in 2005, remembering my experience in basketball camp when I was 16, I started my own basketball program for special needs children. Just like Mighty Mike, I believe everyone can "bounce back," no matter what challenges life brings us. Epilepsy is one of those challenges. It affects millions throughout the world, but it doesn't have to slow you down. Many well-known people in history have had epilepsy: the emperor Julius Caesar, the painter Vincent Van Gogh, and the writer Charles Dickens are all thought to have had epilepsy.

Signing autographs is one of my favorite parts of my new job. Sometimes I get to sign an autograph for a kid with epilepsy. I always tell them that I hope watching me play shows them that they can also do special things. One girl asked me if I still took my medications, and I told her I do—10 pills every night before I go to bed.

I might not be able to sign a poster for you or give you one of my basketballs, but I'd like to share some coaching tips—things I've learned about epilepsy and about bouncing back. Here's one that my father told me: "Limits do not define you, but you define your limits." The next part of the book is all about how you define yourself—tips and tricks for understanding your epilepsy and taking control of your thoughts, so that epilepsy is always what you have, and not who you are.

Time Out

Feeling Different

As a young person with epilepsy, you may feel different or alone, and might even be bullied at school because of your epilepsy. If you haven't experienced this—super! There's no reason to think that you will. But if you've ever felt different because of a personal struggle, you may need to spend some time practicing self-confidence and learning to control unhelpful thoughts.

You are special and capable of great things, but unhelpful thoughts can hold you back and sabotage your self-confidence. There are lots of ways to keep such thoughts on the bench. Make a list of some of the problems you're having because of unhelpful thinking. Try to notice every time you have an unhelpful thought about yourself: Catch yourself doing it. Make a list of some things you can do when you've caught yourself thinking negatively. Maybe it would help to remember that about 3 million Americans have epilepsy, and that many great people in the history of the world have had epilepsy (and other conditions) and it has not held them back one bit. Or maybe you can practice giving yourself a pep talk that focuses on the positive, unique things about you—practice with a parent or friend when you're not feeling down, so you'll know what to say to yourself when you do start thinking this way.

If the pressure ever gets unbearable, talk with an adult, like your parents, a teacher, your doctor, a psychologist, or your school counselor.

Handling Seizures

Because seizures are unpredictable, handling them is a two-part process: It takes action and teamwork.

First, live a healthy lifestyle. Eat healthy foods. Take your medication. Get proper rest. Listen to your doctors. And be active. The more active you are, the better you will feel. If you worry about having seizures while exercising, talk to your doctors about safe ways to get moving.

Second, be prepared. Educate family, schoolmates, teammates, and friends about what to do to help protect you should a seizure happen. You will not only help others to feel more secure, but you will also help yourself. It's OK to be selective about who you want to tell your story to, and remember that your true friends will be your true friends through both good times and bad.

Worrying and Fear

You never know when seizures are going to happen. It's like you're living on the edge all the time. Experiencing worry and fear is normal. But there's plenty you can do to keep your mental attitude positive even while you're worried.

Recognizing that you're experiencing fear is important. Name it, and try to figure out what is making you feel that way. Worrying that you'll get hurt is very different from worrying about what your classmates will think if they see you have a seizure, and those are both different from worrying that you won't be able to do something you want to do because of epilepsy.

Once you know what is making you worried, you can start a list of things that might help you be less afraid or stay positive through your fear. Talking to the people around you about what you're worried about or afraid of is a great place to start, and they can probably recommend some things for you to do to help you with any fears and worries. Also, acting as if you're not afraid (even though you are!) can be a great way to start to feel better.

Another important thing to remember is that worry and fear

are telling you things about the situation you're in. Ask yourself if you're worried because something dangerous, and not just scary, is going on.

You can't control your emotions or the tough times in your life, but how you act on them is a great measure of your own inner growth and strength. Epilepsy is something you live with, but it's not something you have to suffer from. If you can be open and honest with yourself, then your friends and family will be honest in return. Sure, questions and worries may arise, but try not to be afraid to talk to someone, especially your doctor and parents. You can feel good!

Staying Positive

Living with epilepsy gives you so much to think about. It also gives you a lot of responsibility—more than most kids. It can be easy to get overwhelmed or sad, especially after a seizure. Everyone tells you that you're fine, but your body might feel weak, you might be embarrassed because the seizure happened in front of friends, and you be sad and not want to talk to anyone. It can be hard to know what to say or how to think after a seizure.

First, know things can and will get better. There are lots of things you can do to make sure life is fun, and you can take steps to make sure things get better for you. It can take some practice to stay positive, though.

One thing to practice is helpful self-talk. When you catch yourself thinking unhelpful things about yourself or your life, try to switch to more helpful, encouraging thoughts. Pay attention to your internal thoughts and notice what words make you feel bad about yourself, and what words make you feel good. Try switching the unhelpful words to helpful ones—for example, tell yourself "I can try," instead of "I can't." Some kids even write out pep talks for themselves so that they can read them when they're discouraged or not so positive about things. It's also helpful to visualize good things happening.

One of the most important tricks to staying positive is to find someone to talk to about what you are feeling and what you are thinking. The more you talk and communicate with people, the better you're likely to feel.

Another great way to stay positive is to get involved in some activities you like—sports, music, the school newspaper, or anything healthy that you enjoy. We all have gifts and talents. Find out what yours is, develop it and use it, and watch others smile.

Thinking positively about yourself and your life is an important factor in bouncing back from any of life's problems or adversities, so it's a great skill to practice.

Triple-Threat Breakdown

How do you deal with adversity? In your lifetime, you'll deal with different types of problems, troubles, and things that make you struggle, also known as adversity. Epilepsy is certainly one of those challenges, and dealing with it can sometimes be lonely. You're not alone: This section can help you deal with adversity and score and win with epilepsy.

Step 1. Find an Outlet

We all have things we're good at. These things are positive outlets. You may be good in science, math, art, or a specific sport. Challenging yourself to work hard at those things can make you feel energized and can help you replace negative self-talk with positive thoughts and actions.

- What are some problems Mike faced in the story?
- How did Mike deal with adversity?
- What was Mike's outlet? How did he find it?
- How can you help a friend who is struggling to find an outlet?
- What is your outlet? And how can you grow from it?

Step 2. Communicate

One of the most essential elements to overcoming life's obstacles is communication. It is always good to talk about your troubles to people you know and trust. This is not a cure, but it can help you feel at ease and stronger.

- Find an example in the story where Mike communicates how he feels to someone. How does that help him feel more comfortable?
- Find an example of another character in the story who grows closer to Mike by just talking with him. Why do you think that happens?
- What are some ways you can practice communicating with people around you?

Step 3. Be a Good Teammate

Being a kid and managing homework, chores, and friends can be tough. If you have seizures, that list of pressures gets bigger. It can make your head seem like it's spinning. When you are dealing with problems, it can be better to go into a battle with a friend or two. It's important to know how to be a good teammate, like Mike's teammates are in the story. If you have epilepsy, or if you have a friend who has epilepsy, it's especially important to know how to deal with adversity that's both physical and emotional.

- In the story, who is on Mike's team—who is there to help him deal with problems? What are some things they do to show Mike that they're good teammates?
- If you have epilepsy, think about who you want on your team. Who do you tell that you have the condition?
- If you don't have epilepsy, how would you help a classmate who has it?
- In the story, Mike deals with a bully. Have you ever been bullied? How did it make you feel? What would you do if you noticed someone being bullied on the playground?

Post-Game Wrap Up

Seizure Types

There are many different types of seizures. People may experience just one type or more than one. The kind of seizure a person has depends on which part and how much of the brain is affected by the electrical disturbance that produces seizures. Experts divide seizures into generalized seizures (absence, atonic, tonic-clonic, myoclonic), partial (simple and complex) seizures, nonepileptic seizures, and status epilepticus.

Primary Generalized Seizures

Absence seizure (formerly called petit mal)
generalized seizure most common in children; a lapse in consciousness with a blank stare that begins and ends within a few seconds. May be accompanied by rapid eye blinking or chewing movements.

Atonic seizure (drop attack)
generalized seizure where sudden, complete loss of muscle control and balance results in collapse.

Tonic-clonic
most conspicuous type of seizure; generalized seizures which usually begin with a sudden cry, fall, and rigidity (tonic phase), followed by muscle jerks, shallow breathing, or temporarily suspended breathing and change in skin color (clonic phase), possible loss of bladder or bowel control; seizure usually lasts a couple of minutes, followed by confusion and fatigue.

Myoclonus
usually generalized seizures causing massive rapid clonic spasms of a muscle or group of muscles.

Partial Seizures

Simple partial seizure
seizure activity in one part of the brain resulting in: a) jerking in

one area of the body, arm, leg or face; b) partial sensory seizures where a patient experiences distorted environments, sensory illusion, or gastric discomfort. The motor or sensory activity may progress to a convulsive seizure.

Complex partial seizure

usually starts with a blank stare, followed by random activity. Person appears unaware of surroundings, seems dazed and mumbles, is unresponsive, clumsy. When seizure ends, post-ictal confusion often follows, and the person has no memory of what happened during the seizure. This type of seizure activity is localized mainly to one part of the brain.

Nonepileptic and Status Epilepticus Seizures

Nonepileptic seizures

have a psychological cause or are due to a sudden drop in blood pressure, low blood sugar, or another temporary condition.

Status Epilepticus

severe, potentially life-threatening non-stop seizures, not always related to epilepsy; status epilepticus can result from acute brain injury.

* All information is courtesy of The Epilepsy Foundation of America's website. For further information log onto www.epilepsyfoundation.org.

What To Do During a Seizure

T: Turn the person having a seizure on his or her side.

R: Remove harmful objects from the area.

U: Use something soft under his or her head.

S: Stay calm.

T: Time the seizure. If the person has never had a seizure, or if the seizure lasts longer than five minutes, or if there are more than two seizures, call 911.

fold here

Don't hold the person down or try to stop his or her movements. Do not try to force the mouth open with any hard object or with your fingers. A person having a seizure cannot swallow his or her tongue. Efforts to hold the tongue down can injure teeth or jaw.

About the Authors

Robert Skead

Robert Skead is the author of several popular sports books for children. When he's not crafting stories, Robert can often be found at schools speaking with children and adults about creative writing and the importance of discovering one's talents for a fulfilled life. Through these author visits, Robert speaks to more than 5,000 students per year.

He lives with his wife and family in New Jersey.

For more information about his writing workshops, visit www.robertskead.com.

Mike "Mighty Mike" Simmel

Mike "Mighty Mike" Simmel is a professional show basketball player with the world-famous Harlem Wizards, where he's played since 2001. He has been a featured performer at hundreds of halftime shows, camps, and school assemblies throughout the country. Mike performs in front of millions of people and audiences all across America. He is also one of three million Americans living with epilepsy.

Standing only 5 feet, 9 inches tall, Mike is your typical "boy next door," who has used his gifts and work ethic to make his dreams in basketball come true. A 1996 graduate of Don Bosco Prep (Ramsey, NJ), Mike was an honor-roll student, three-year varsity starter, and standout point guard, winning All-League Honors. He was captain of the team as a senior. Mike is a graduate of Purchase College

(SUNY), where he was a two-year team captain and led the team in both assists and steals.

The former New York Knicks ball boy has performed in front of crowds both big and small: on stage at the Apollo Theater, live on NBC television, in front of crowds at NBA and college halftimes, and in gymnasiums and at special events all over the country, including the 2009 Men's NCAA Final Four. Since 1998, he has lectured and performed at nearly 450 basketball camps across the country.

In addition to his role as a principal dribbler with the Wizards, Mike serves as a national spokesperson for epilepsy awareness and has spoken on behalf of the Epilepsy Foundation of America and its affiliates at many events and summer camps across the country. Each year, he speaks and performs at the Epilepsy Foundation's National Kids Speak Up! and U.S. Public Policy Institute in Washington, DC. Mike was also selected as a national spokesperson for two major pharmaceutical companies: Eisai Pharmaceuticals (2004–2006) and Abbott Laboratories (2006–2007).

Mike constantly looks to donate his time and talents to encouraging and advocating for people, especially children, who have epilepsy and other disabilities. He started his own non-profit organization, the Bounce Out the Stigma Project, Inc., to help empower young people and educate the public. Mike's summer basketball camps for children with special needs, now in their 6th year, are highly successful and are in full partnership with the Epilepsy Foundation of New Jersey. In addition, his signature assembly programs to educate young people about epilepsy in schools are a bona-fide success.

Mighty Mike has been featured in many news publications and on regional and local television, including FOX, PBS, CBS College Sports Network, MSG Sports, and RNN News for his outstanding efforts both on the basketball court and in the community. He has also been featured on many radio shows across the country, including Radio Disney, ESPN Radio, voiceamerica.com, and Bloomberg Radio.

In 2002, Mighty Mike won the Pepsi Sports Award for achievements on the court and in the community. In August 2007, Mike was honored with *Exceptional Parent* magazine's Maxwell J. Schleifer Distinguished Service Award for his work within the special needs community in front of more than 50,000 fans at Yankee Stadium during Disability Awareness Night. In May 2009, Mike was presented with the New Jersey Governor's Recreation and Commission on Individuals for Disabilities Award for Exemplary Lifestyle and Education Award. Also in 2009, he was honored in Orlando, Florida, by the United States Junior Chamber of Commerce (Jaycees) with the TOYA (Ten Outstanding Young Americans) Award. Previous winners of this prestigious award have included ex-presidents.

For more information about Mighty Mike Simmel and information on how to join his fan club, visit mightymikebasketball.com.

About Magination Press
Magination Press publishes self-help books for kids and the adults in their lives. Magination Press in an imprint of the American Psychological Association, the largest scientific and professional organization representing psychologists in the United States and the largest association of psychologists worldwide.